Underwater Panther

Poems
by Angie Macri

Winner 2014 Cowles Poetry Book Prize

Southeast Missouri State University Press | 2015

Underwater Panther by Angie Macri
Winner 2014 Cowles Poetry Book Prize
Copyright 2015: Angie Macri

Softcover: 978-0-9962596-1-3
$14.00

First published in 2015 by
Southeast Missouri State University Press
One University Plaza, MS 2650
Cape Girardeau, MO 63701
www.semopress.com

Cover art:
Bow and Arrow by Katherine Strause
48" x 36"
oil on canvas
in the collection of the Central Arkansas Library System
Katherine Strause is a working artist and educator. She exhibits nationally and has work in many public and private collections. Ms. Strause is currently Chair of the Art Department and Associate Professor of Painting at Henderson State University.

Cover design: Carrie M. Walker

Library of Congress Cataloging-in-Publication Data

Macri, Angie.
 [Poems. Selections]
 Underwater panther : poems / by Angie Macri.
    pages cm
 Includes bibliographical references and index.
 ISBN 978-0-9962596-1-3 (pbk. : alk. paper)
 I. Title.
PS3613.A28333A6 2015
811'.6--dc23
                            2015021618

*for my mother, Barbara
and for my father, Jim*

Contents

9   Inheriting Pressure

I.

13   Arimipichia
14   Immaculate Conception
15   Lost to Fever
16   The Story of Her Shore
17   American Beauty
18   The *Genny*
20   Least Tern
21   Ten-Year Drought
23   The Bell at Kaskaskia
24   Singing Colossus
25   The Heart of a River Never Is Its Own
26   Tornado at Chester

II.

29   Black Code
30   Heartland
31   Cahokia Seedling
32   Marie Jeanne
34   Marie Louise
36   Marie Scypion
39   Thebes Courthouse
40   Thou hast brought a vine out of Egypt:

III.

45   Veins and Coal Fields
47   So Far Now from the Sea
48   First Road through Sparta
49   Sparta
50   North of Sparta
51   Jones and Nesbitt Mine, Coulterville
52   Roseborough Mine, Sparta

53	Stripping Shovel
54	Green Dragon
55	Stone Box Cemetery
56	Unweaved:
57	Under Mayapples
58	Watershed
60	Good Times, Bad Times

IV.

65	Acceleration
66	The Fathers Who Never Seem to Speak
67	Cadence
69	Flight Pattern
71	Venus
72	Tongue of Vines
73	Wish to His Branch
74	Lines and Glass Insulators
75	Myocarditis
76	Cathedral Train
78	Galette des Rois
80	Cerulean
81	Low in Spirits
82	The Height Is the Only Place that Will Do
83	Relict of a Husband, Daughter of a General
85	Ismenian Dragon
86	Ourania, Pandemos, Apostrophia
87	Hephaestus's Fire
88	Notes
90	About the Author

Acknowledgments

Grateful acknowledgment is made to the editors and readers of the following journals in which poems in this collection have appeared or are forthcoming, sometimes in slightly different form:

Birmingham Poetry Review	"Lost to Fever"
The Boiler	"Unweaved"
Cave Wall	"American Beauty," "Arimipichia"
Central Arkansas Broadside Project	"Lines and Glass Insulators"
The Chaffin Journal	"Stone Box Cemetery"
Cincinnati Review	"Jones and Nesbitt Mine, Coulterville," "Roseborough Mine, Sparta"
Crab Orchard Review	"Inheriting Pressure"
Crazyhorse	"Green Dragon," "Watershed"
The Dos Passos Review	"Immaculate Conception," "North of Sparta," "Sparta"
Ecotone	"Tornado at Chester"
Faultline	"First Road through Sparta"
Fugue	"So Far Now from the Sea"
Limestone	"Least Tern"
The Lindenwood Review	"Good Times, Bad Times"
Lullwater Review	"Acceleration"
Natural Bridge	"Black Code," "Cahokia Seedling," "Flight Pattern," "Veins and Coal Fields"
New Delta Review	"The Bell at Kaskaskia," "Heartland"
The Pinch	"Cathedral Train," "The Story of Her Shore"
Prime Mincer	"Galette des Rois"
Quiddity	"Stripping Shovel"
Redactions: Poetry & Poetics	"Under Mayapples"
RHINO	"Ourania, Pandemos, Apostrophia"
Salamander	"The Heart of a River Never Is Its Own," "Cadence," "Ten-Year Drought"
San Pedro River Review	"Singing Colossus"
Slant	"The *Genny*"
South Dakota Review	"Tongue of Vines," "Wish to His Branch"
Southern Indiana Review	"The Fathers Who Never Seem to Speak"
Sugar House Review	"Cerulean," "Low in Spirits"
Tar River Poetry	"Ismenian Dragon"
Third Coast	"Hephaestus's Fire," "Thebes Courthouse"

I appreciate those who helped make this book possible: Pattiann Rogers, Heather Ross Miller, Phillip Bartell, Joan Dudley, Amy Baldwin, Sandy Longhorn, Caroline Lewis, Yolanda Mitchell, Antoinette Brim, Joey Cole, my students at Pulaski Technical College, Hope Coulter, Katrina Vandenberg, Stacey Lynn Brown, Lyndsey Daniel, Nick Boone, Allison Joseph and Jon Tribble, Patti and John Prusila, Mark and Christy Leckband, John Elms, Theodore Michalk, Larry and Sharon McBride, Randall Schopfer, and all who valued art and place and took the time to help me find my way.

Special thanks to the Arkansas Arts Council for an individual artist fellowship, to Kathy Strause for a sure-shot cover, and to Susan Swartwout, Dixon Hearne, and Southeast Missouri State University Press for giving this book its space.

To all my friends and family who let me sketch them in these poems, including Becky Bumann Trost, Cheryl Heuman Suedmeyer, Tanutda Pittayathikhun Devine, Rick and Ruby Kohlman Caudle, Barbara Grah Rinehart, Donald Grah, Opal Marie Bollinger Grah, and Illinois Country, what we were and are, I give this book, my love.

And to my husband Wade and our beloved children Clementine, Jack, Jude, and Sidra, who help me find my way home.

Inheriting Pressure

As the sliding of cat's shoulders, the sky stalked
above my father's cotton shirt, ringed with sweat

and lined on the back where the blades came together
as a moth's wings. The storm built in a tempo

that I knew, beat into heart rate and soil: Gorham
gone with Murphysboro's children, downburst

plowing with a wide noise. They recited such stories
of the Tri-State Tornado or the funnel that took

the Chester Bridge two summers after my mother
was born, but when my time came, it was unlike clouds

that boiled along the horizon. First came the thrum
like a train rising up the hill from the Kaskaskia,

then the tulip tree reaching to me in supplication
and my father running to the cellar from the fields.

> You will go, down in the earth, under topsoil, subsoil
> and minerals, deep roots in rocks and bedrock, solid
>
> and hidden. You will press along the north wall
> where the furnace stands idle. The beams above
>
> will breathe with the wind of it. As the heart contracts
> and empties, blood echoes in the chambers, and you will
>
> force under green darkness, listening to the churn,
> learning the lack of key and order. In the dark
>
> powerless nights that follow, you will feel night roll
> down your sides with the salt that was once in your body.

I.

Arimipichia

Underwater so they wouldn't set the world on fire,
the panthers made their way. The rumors of cougars
aren't lost on us now. The state can say what it may,
but the great cat hit along the Mississippi by a train
crawled into the lawn of the Menard House to die,

and we saw it like a meteor, licking paws of sky. Cattle
are mauled, we know, by no other claws, and tracks
in mud don't lie. Where the soil smells of blood
after a rain when the fields have just been plowed,
steel casting into iron to sow the seeds, a cougar

walks the tracks in Riley Lake as a matter of course,
over a hundred pounds and full of fawn. Horses
feel its stealth sure as deer forage at dawn or hawks
spiral in red or timber rattlers from Rockwood
south master the hills until the first hard freeze.

Black panther on the bluff above the prison target range,
golden cougars near Ellis Grove, they mean change
and disorder. This cougar died on its side while
the thunder moon untied the river over Kaskaskia.
We come to see so no one can say otherwise.

Immaculate Conception

We count by the Mississippi
where we grow up, the span of the river
the time between lightning and thunder,

one-Mississippi, two-Mississippi, three,
the space of the word as the distance
between power and its sound.

You can see storms hours away
in Missouri, brewing before they cross
the river, the Mississippi, father

of waters, old man, holy spirit, immaculate
conception, yes, a virgin in cloth
of gold, a girl with a twist of hips

that as a woman will unwind,
all curves and bends and deep
places you just can't see

unless you know. In summer
storms, she moves like a figure liquid
in stone, the kind of marble

that has a quality of life, hands open
at her sides. We count by her,
emphasizing each syllable like curls.

She lets her skirts rub along the land
and gives the soil its way to yield, taking
her own sweet time, crest and recede.

Lost to Fever

The cemeteries that flow in certain rivers,
catholic and protestant, hold children
christened and lost to fever, their names
still in papers stacked in the courthouse

on the hill. Buried with bells, now lost
in canopies of grapes, with the river's crush
in times of flood, they are left without cedar
or stone. The moon shone as day, bright

as mirrors, bright as bones that flesh
had come off of centuries before. Men dug
the graves up to try to save them to the bluff.
Now pallid sturgeon are followed by sonar

in this place. The pecans the French loved,
the voyagers and fathers, the set statements
of the stars, the voices in song—the scissors
cut through those unrolled bolts of cloth

into a pattern. The river crossed the surface
of the soil like hands before a body, a child
playing at being blind, exploring by fingertips,
rapid and devoted. To the wrists, and then

the shoulders, the land began moving. Men
got too close to the chasm and had to be rescued
from the trees. Bright as sturgeons pressed
close to the river's bed, as barn roofs in the moon

on the floodplain, as cottonwood seeds,
children lost to fever move with silt to the sea.

The Story of Her Shore

With the text of a breath, the Mississippi
reads her shore, and voices like pins
drop on the floor, absorbed
by the sky under which they fall
even as they scatter in wings
and acres.

From the bluff, people watched the houses
fall, the river having made up her mind
which way to run. Neither door
nor foundation was any match
for her stamina.

She made her bed and she lay
down in it, breathing in willows
and cottonwoods, chimney bricks
and windows. Open eyes
crushed shut
from right angles.

The orchards, the penetrating roots
of roses rubbed along her back
as she stretched out, relaxed
and wide. The clouds opened
as white as the mouth
of the snake, and she slid by
into cotton.

American Beauty

Sky of roses, blood out from bone,
in the beat of thorns, the sweet
traps under leaves from the blooms
like sleep in afternoon, wandering.

In his garden where I am small,
all my fingers fit between the thorns.
I put my nose in every face, holding
the stems of crooked bones in recitation

of the names I learn: Blue Moon,
Iceberg, Chrysler Imperial,
American Beauty. He planted
these for his wife for his time away

on the rivers. His large hands
summon them to grow, like echoes
of his voice, like clear desire. The slur
of bees is an atlas to my ears.

After a rain, they hang their heads
with the weight of the arm
of our galaxy, and I walk between,
not touching. He worked the rivers,

knew their bends, their pull,
moving up and down each in steam
and humidity on the dredge
Ste. Genevieve, from Cairo to St. Paul,

from St. Louis to Omaha, from Cairo
to Pittsburgh. Deckhand, leverman,
first mate, he was weeks away
with the velocity of the river, the speed

of the dredge, and she waited in the elbows,
the bends, the eddies of roses.

The Genny

The tap of starlight, like fingers on a sweating glass,
this is the night up from the river's face, up against
velvet space. From the dredge, he could see this all.

He worked the cutter head, the inlet to the pump,
the trencher and the teeth as it chewed, managing
torque, moving debris and silt from the waterways.

With Morse code, they spoke. The boiler ran hot
as August's belly, but the Texas deck might catch
a breeze. What is my heart's desire? To ride her

through the dark or fog without striking
something else, three hundred pounds of copper and tin
ringing in her bell, but the river's no place for children.

Pull of the mud, soft as old flesh, the cubic yards
per hour pace with the soundings that he took,
working with the crew to clear the channel bars.

Home, he pressed wine from his grape arbor
between the house and the roses he planted
for his wife. Like clotted veils, the grapes weren't

good for tasting, he warned, only for wine
in time, and I believed him, letting the tendrils curl
around mine. He spoke little of the *Genny* by then.

He served me lemonade he mixed, sweeter
than anything I'd ever had, sweating
into my fingers wrapped around my glass.

He worked his dog, teasing me about squirrel stew.
She wasn't a pet, but for hunting. She sat beautiful
under his pecan. Alchemist, Radiance, Dame de Coeur,

he dusted the roses and brought in buds
for his wife to force. I waited in the rows, hands
back from what was his, following paths he had

made decades before. Even from the old well
off their back porch, I could see the roses swelling,
petals that I might take if they fell to the ground.

Least Tern

The least tern breeds where it scrapes the sand,
shallow in the river sun. Mississippi, Ohio, Missouri,
it hovers before it dives.
                        The least tern courts
using river shiners, the male flying with the fish,
the females following his call, and he picks one to feed
on the ground, a pair bond.
                          The least tern creates
a colony, hundreds beside each other in summer's
stomach of warm pebbles and soil, Mosenthein
Island by St. Louis, Bell Island near Shawneetown.

Both male and female tend the nest, using
their bodies to make shade. During heat waves,
they wet themselves in the river to cool their eggs.

In a day, traders could harvest over a thousand
terns for ladies' hats, and most nests have gone
with dredging, channels, flooding. At Baldwin,

a few least terns have been seen. The power plant
burns Wyoming coal, cooling its boilers with a shallow
lake made from the Kaskaskia floodplain. Some

mornings you can see its plumes from home. First
in the state, thirtieth in the nation, carbon dioxide
releases to the atmosphere.
                              The least tern might try
to nest in its waste ash. Not finding sandbars
isolated from riverbanks,
                      they are lured to nest
on barges at Alton, an island built by the Corps
covered with gravel and sand.
                         From twelve nests,
twenty hatch, down colored as sand with black flecks.
The least tern always hatches with open eyes.

Ten-Year Drought

Arrowleaves and spring beauties, roots
we might eat, bloom in the rush of spring,

but this is summer, and the fields break
apart in pentagons, hexagons, deep cracks,

as if the sun has stamped down. The sleepy
duskywing moves between in the iridescence

of dew under the beaten copper sky
of morning. At one time, the Kaskaskia

unrolled kettles and cut the metal into bells
that rung with the beads of the living

and in the graves. We still find remnants
of their camp now, although not as often when

it's so dry. The best time is after a rain
and in the spring, in the plow's parallels.

But this is summer, hung, heavy as the bell
on the Island. Like the ground, it holds

a crack. It was moved away from the old town,
but the river still sometimes knocks it down.

The prison is on the horizon, shimmering
in heat waves. In places you can find stains

from high water, the river's crest on silos
that didn't buckle. The river has always liked

to roll to the west into the edge of her old bed,
from when ice once carved the valley, in buffalo,

in corn. Now she runs mighty low,
and the dredge must scrape a way for the coal,

for the grain. We walk, our ankles powdered
with sulfur like sunlight ground up into ounces

in a paper bag, bought at the hardware store. This
is the ten-year drought, and no one seems to worry.

The Bell at Kaskaskia

Songbirds leave for Mexico, flying by night
for fear of hawks, turning by stars. The wrens
stay. Streets of persimmon, poplar, pear, crossed
with independence, elm, and pecan plot under
river now. On the Island, out from St. Mary
on winding oil roads, I know I'll find little
at the end of La Grande Rue.

Think of the river as flowing stone, shoving
shoulders, picking fingers. Farmers find bones,
skulls, stones sometimes, cast out of the old
graves, Aco, Rouensa, Ste. Gemme Beauvais
alike. Their bell hangs in egrets and grasshoppers,
lily in thorns. My mother, grandmother all heard
it ring every Fourth.

It took every flood but the last, falling in '93,
cracking. Underseepage, saturation, sandboils,
the six-hundred foot levee break was not a breach,
the Corps said. They were not there, running, soil,
water erupting. The sheriff tried to save
swimming livestock in his boat. Mud rose
to ceilings, silos buckled.

Heat swells the Commons, soybean and corn
sprouting in my paces. From France where it
was cast in 1741, from its two years coming
upriver from New Orleans by rope and hand
on bateau, the bell stays. The wrens nest
in moss, bark, and snakeskin, in breakable clouds
and rampant chords.

Singing Colossus

The pinnacles in the Mississippi mark the upper
edge of the old gulf. You can imagine the sea reaching
this far, as warm as dragon hide. In Egypt at Thebes,
a stone voice sang each morning as the sun warmed
the rock. Here, so that barges could navigate in times
of drought, the Corps drilled and blasted the limestone
apart. We moved away from questions of sphinxes,
from temples of air and light, running rails and arches
over the river with cantilever and anchor spans
in pinned trusses. When we came back to try to answer,
to thin courthouse columns, to Spar Hawk's Landing,
when we found the mouth of the dead and put an alabaster
cup to what was left so they could finally drink,
we found we had nowhere left to be.

The Heart of a River Never Is Its Own

River of faith, coal from the mines, and fur
and grain and war, all men and women's longing,
these aren't the river's dreams. Remember,
she doesn't dream. She works the shore like dough
that will rise and bake in the first hours of morning
at Kaskaskia, Ste. Genevieve, Prairie du Rocher.
We played while the adults would talk
of her stages, and then we ate from the ovens, spread
out in the shade like her body, with the glory
of light reflected off moving water.

Cities were born and died but farms
lasted forever if well tended. No tools
rusted if you used them. Barges
murmured back and forth to the sea.
Here Menard, Indian agent, had won the trust
and trade, and his name fixed on the last profit
that we knew, the prisons where criminals
were sent downstate to do their time
in the perimeters our men guarded.
My uncle told stories sometimes of those
inside, the murderers, the boy with stardust
in his eyes. Child, that could be you.

The heart of a river never is its own.
Measure the length and depth, the gauges
on bridges and shores, and the tones
of trains run north and south on gentle
grades. We tore the bread with our hands
after asking Jesus to come, to be our guest.
We ate fast, then counted the steps down
to the Menard house, the Indian trail now set
with railroad ties into the hill, coming out
of the woods by his smokehouse, called
the slavehouse then, where rosemary still grows.

Tornado at Chester

Through the lightning of early morning,
the colonel saw the clouds.
One was the river suspended.
The other was muscle surrounding bone.
Great soldiers, he said to them,
where is my home?
In the waters, said the river.
In the bluffs, said the muscle on bone.
And the colonel, who was listening
to his town spinning around him,
saw the clouds lift the ferryboat
from the riverside, its engine, boiler,
smokestack thrown up the bluff
with the broken sounds of battles at Thames
and Bad Axe. Great soldiers, he said,
where is my home?
In the waters, said the river.
In the bluffs, said the muscle on bone.
Through the lightning of early morning
with houses gutted of greenbacks and beds,
the colonel saw the clouds,
churches, barns, and legs
held in the broken arms of dawn.

II.

Black Code

A man is a hand
                  around a pan, an axe
where the animals licked the earth,
      where the tribes made solar salt
and discarded shards still bear fabric prints.
          At Half Moon Lick and Great Salt Spring,
near Eagle Mountain, a thousand hands
          chop wood for furnaces and boil brine in iron kettles.

A man is the land
                with work no free man
would do. Trees fall. Heat boils past breath
       while the hawk hunts in its circles. The beetle
walks by the underwater panthers drawn on the rocks.
          They build a bank at Shawneetown in Greek
revival style, with a limestone front façade.

A man is the plan.
                  The ferry crosses
from Kentucky at Shawneetown, and the road
       runs up to Equality. Pipes draw from the wells,
the pieces of trees thrust down into dark peaceful places.
         Summer's descent ricochets, traveling along a flame,
bushels to river and road. Eyes fill with half moon
       phases above and the channel below, both hooks,
bound. Illinois' pretty penny builds on the salt lines
         coupled with black laws and iron.

A man is a brand,
                is sand inside his skin,
both those sold and those profiting. The deer hides sell,
         tanned, salt on the flesh side. The augered logs
stretch many miles. For a buck, the fires are tended
       in the trenches, fed, stoked, nurtured,
promoted by these codes through days and nights.

Heartland

I.

At San Domingo, Renault bought five-hundred
slaves and their memories of being traded
on the sea for rum, of growing indigo and sugar.
He took them, his miners from Paris,
and furnace bricks up the Mississippi
to Fort de Chartres in hopes of finding silver.
Just under the soil, they found galena shining,
and so they picked and shoveled near the Saline
and Mine la Motte, muscles searing as fire's heart,
smelting lead ore into collars to hang on horses' necks.
Some days, thunder rolled cannons. The horses
walked through viburnum to Ste. Genevieve.
The ore went by keelboat to New Orleans,
and then to France. It became ammunition there.

II.

You couldn't sleep. You blazed the way
to the river, where seagulls were fluent
in sweet indigo islands. Behind the houses
in town, women in blue grew chives
and yarrow from the alluvial plain. The galena
lay as heavy blankets. The mines yielded more
than a thousand pounds a day. You must
have had names. You might have had a song.
It is something you had known all along,
the trinity, the ring of shovel on bright ore,
the luster like sweat up from the chest of the earth.
You learned every seventh summer swells
with cicada, molting, drumming, nursing
on root juices, digging, and again calling.

Cahokia Seedling

The pear, the belly of a woman,
full, opens rough to the tongue.

Only five of the old French
orchard remain, forty feet tall, three
in diameter. They bear fifteen

bushels each. In the old bed
of the Mississippi, pears end

the size of eggs, their flesh
like sweet sand of the river.
They are picked from skiffs

during the flood. Young trees
die then, the old thriving.

Pears unpeel heavy as sleep
while girls drift in the current
with stars of silt on their feet.

Marie Jeanne

isn't a mother,
isn't leaving the clover
and wild red lilies
of Kaskaskia.

By the judge's words,
she is sent downriver
to the Superior Council
in New Orleans.

It wasn't a baby,
months inside turning
and reaching. No arm
or skull fragments

on a doorstep, no
mouth opened to air,
no blade. She was a slave
of Damoiselle Marie Vincennes,

worth livres and minots
of salt, on one-year lease.
No bell rung for birth
and none for death,

no gauze cap fitted
on wild peach hair.
She didn't kneel into the soil
in the vegetables

of Brazeau's garden,
planted on Good Friday
to bear double, cucumbers
to be eaten with cream.

The grapes along the river
twist high in the trees
so that no one can reach them
or profit from their sweet taste.

Marie Louise

I.

Little is soft here but the newly born,
Ste. Genevieve, Santa Genoveva, Misère.
Mulatto slave Marie Louise has a baby
by Antoine Janis. He lives with her
like she's his wife despite the priest,
his family, a *criminal affair*. The newborn
cries, pulling in air for the first time, eyes
tightly shut against the light, the soft spot
on its crown pulsing like a thunderhead.
The earth utters of lead and buckskin, wheat
and lime, and salt is offered in exchange,
boiled from where the Saline meets the Mississippi.
The river floods and then subsides so that
the fields are full of the silt she leaves behind.

II.

Ste. Genevieve, Santa Genoveva, Misère,
with the magnificence of kings,
the Spanish galiot *La Vigilante* comes
to Illinois country with cannon and guns,
governor and commandant. They talk
of the red scare and salt, fifteen minots
a day. Marie Louise has a second child
by Antoine Janis. He plans to buy her,
so Vital Ste. Gemme Beauvais rents her away.
Janis follows. The governors say no
according to the Royal Decree. The home
of Ste. Gemme Beauvais is whitewashed,
poteaux en terre, cedar set in the ground.
Little is soft here but the newly born.

III.

You will strive to stop the emancipation
of this slave. The river floods the grand fields,
and buckskins protect through underbrush
to the lead mines. Janis has the money
to set Marie Louise free. The children
stain their tongues with raspberries. The river
bears blue cotton shipped up from New Orleans.
They cut the cloth into form with seams,
skirts like sky, the summer kind when
thunderheads seethe. The family bears in mind
the shame of their ruined good name.
Little is soft here but the newly born.
Ste. Genevieve, Santa Genoveva, Misère,
Marie Louise petitions to be free.

Marie Scypion

My father died in the throat of a well
or was sold downriver to New Orleans.
My mother was Natchez, captured in war.
I was born at Fort de Chartres, the blooming
stone of a river shore

                    and became a gift from a priest.
My mistress married a man who built
the first water mill in St. Louis. It turns
still as the constellations,

                    and I show you, three daughters,
Celeste, divine, of the sky,

                    Catiche,
pure, little doll,

                    and Marguerite, my pearl.

With copper cauldrons and troughs
of dough, black walnut cupboards,
vases of oil, gardens

                    of three sisters,
corn, pumpkin, beans, I have raised
everything. My lady dies,
and the auction block is waiting.

Apart from you, may my blood become the Mississippi
that bears grain and fur to the mouth of the sea.

I.

In the droughts of three months,
the first child was born of apples
thick in the boughs, like stars
clustered and ground to cider.

The mother with feet and hands
of Negro shape filled baskets

as gifts, telling stories of frost
too early or late along the river,

fog like thoughts welling
from warm soil. The child
was given to the lady's daughter
who won't let her be sold

and argues she is Natchez
and free but only if she stays
with me. Set free by the court,
then brought back, the wheels

turn by the power of water,
the waste of grain to dust.

II.

The second is *beat, bruised, ill treated*,
hidden for thirty days, her daughter,
granddaughter as well. Chouteau
makes them pay mind. The court
fines him one cent for his action.

She is a drink from a spring, cold
even in the iron summer light.
Every hour is the time
to fight, to press in Latin, writs
of habeas corpus, mandamus,

while the men talk so often of her mother's hair,
its particular curl, like wool.

She would feel this with her sister
curled in sleep.

III.

This child opened from the throat.
She was the one the mother was allowed
to keep. They took salt from the springs
and heat from the mouth

of oven coals. So many times
a plaintiff, she was the one whose case
finally set them all free. Change
of venue took them to a court

held in a store in Herculaneum,
halfway back to where her mother
was born, the property of a priest,
a gift to his cousin, like a gun
or red cauldron. With her mother,
she watched the haze of apples
in bloom and pared them
into form. They lived in limestone

of some ancient sea
full of fossils
no one reads, boundless
life from before.

Thebes Courthouse

We beg our heart not to rise up to testify against us, to tell
no lies in the presence of God. We sit under the elm,
holding court near these unhewn sandstone walls covered
with plaster from native lime and hair. True or not:
the murdered body to the river, Lincoln on the circuit,
Dred Scott in this jail. The sign reads, *He was a fugitive slave
for whom the judge's decision was made establishing a negro's right
to his own person.* In Little Egypt, a dark-eyed girl waits.
She looks for the city of one-hundred gates, dynamite
and gun cotton, poplar cut for the gunnels of keelboats.
An earthquake moved the Ohio to its present bed and sent
the Mississippi on its sharp bend here. Those who know
say it's just a matter of time. The dungeon was turned
into a coal and wood bin. You weigh our heart in your hand.

Thou hast brought a vine out of Egypt:

thou hast cast out the heathen, and planted it
where mounds used to swell until farmed down,
where arrowheads still work their way up, flint
common as sky, as wood.

Thou preparest room before it (the vine),
and didst cause it to take deep root
with deer skins and long lots
that bore wheat. They marked time
with a bell brought upriver hand
over fist on bateau. It was lost
to floods more than once, yet found,

and it (the vine) filled the land.
We traced back those names, LaBrier,
Montroy, Doza, Picou. Mass
was said for French and Kaskaskia
and all mixed blood.

The hills were covered with the shadow
of it, and the boughs thereof were like
the goodly cedars. Like faience, powdered
quartz with soda and copper, like
olivine and serpentinite,

she sent out her boughs unto the sea,
and her branches unto the river.
Fur and tons of wheat went to New Orleans,
and the bell, like a shell, recalled
the ocean.

Why hast thou then broken down her hedges,
so that all they which pass by the way
do pluck her? The black land, Kemet,
forms the fields, the red land, Desheret,
is desert. The land of the living is

to the east, with the land of the dead
in the Island to the west.

The boar out of the wood doth waste it,
and the wild beast of the field doth devour it.
The levee rings the Island and the few homes
left, the church, the courthouse moved
brick by brick from the old place. A gold
cross presses the sky.

Return, we beseech thee, O God of hosts,
look down from heaven, and behold, and visit
this vine. The river backwaters over
streets few recall, the Mississippi
in her course of black steatite.

And the vineyard which thy right hand
hath planted, and the branch that thou madest
strong for thyself, and the broken frames,
and the pecans, the songs sung once
in French, and then in Kaskaskia,

it is burned with fire, it is cut down:
they perish at the rebuke of thy countenance.
We have found the bills of sale, transcribed
into a state database online. In times
of drought, the silt from the river forms
a polished stone.

Let thy hand be upon the man
of thy right hand, upon the son of man
whom thy madest strong for thyself,
the shabti, the slaves, who call for us
from the fields, from the sand
to the east and the west.

So will not we go back from thee:
quicken us, and we will call upon thy name
as we retrace the old foundations

in the downtown, as we meet the open
space where the ferry worked
in the summer's power of snakes,
in the winter when they are more likely
to be sleeping and the river is running
low, embroidered with ice. We find names
like glass trade beads, immaculate,
separate, often blue.

Turn us again, O Lord God of hosts,
cause thy face to shine; and we
shall be saved.

III.

Veins and Coal Fields

From the bottom of a bottle, from the shaft
of a knife, in dark clef of the melodeon's reeds,
they dig and haul Big Muddy coal from Jackson County.
Tamaroa coal runs to Chester on the rails
and then from Belleville to Carondelet.

> The panther screams in the tooth's shadow,
> and the wing band on the hawk runs black as well.

Voices are long on the prairie and short below.
The Herrin coal seam stands six feet in places.
Strip, drift, slope, shaft, open pit, room and pillar,
longwall, they move with toothed shovels
around Schuline. Hopper cars fill from fern fields.

> Black Beauty, Crystal, Home Fire, Gracie, River King,
> five-hundred hives yield a thousand pounds of honey.

Lagoons became shallow, to swamps, bogs,
and marshes. Horsetails, club mosses, ferns,
palms and their pollen layered, covered, pressed
down, dry to flood. We were near the equator then.
There is more heat per pound from such veins.

> Geese meet near abandoned rock to nest,
> and cedars grow with crows from deep down stone.

We fish for striped bass in the lake at the power plant
at Baldwin. Nitrogen oxide and carbon dioxide,
turbines, crushers, grinders, feeders, cyclones, blowers,
fly ash piping, sulfur, chain drives play in the bellows
through the reeds. We know Bloody Williamson.

> In Sparta, some miners pocket pyrite suns
> from the veins of shale and slate above the coal.

We can burn to ash. We can pull it back
into the face of the sun. The dust washes off,
eventually, back into the soil with its old oiled smell.
Like kohl on the eyes, like songbirds breathing
in cages, railroad crossing bells mark nights by the hour.

>We take our power, from strata, from Streamline,
>from muscle with diesel, steam, and iron.

So Far Now from the Sea

In the earth at Rosiclare,
fluorite spreads forty feet wide in crystals
of black-blue cubes, formed when hot water rose
from low in the earth into limestone along rift zones.
Water from the planet deep honeymoons
with stone placed by the sea.

In the earth at Waterloo,
farmers find goniatite fossils that once
swam with tentacles, with good eyes, shells
zigzagging with growth in each of their sutures.
Creatures from one epoch marry wheat fields
so far now from the sea.

In the earth at Sparta,
children catch fireflies that carry light. At the portals,
their fathers go down shafts in cages for their shifts. They
bolt the roof and set the longwall to spin its drum, taking
all in its way. The children's hands glow
and foam with silent sea.

First Road through Sparta

Young trees lean under the sleet, and two men
bend them farther down to mark their way.
They are hauling salt made in the south.
They have worked kettles over fires, harvesting
salt like stars from the sky. At the springs
by the Ohio, mastodons once licked the ground,
and then the buffalo. In winter, tribes came
to hunt and gather salt, evaporating it in pans
of clay strengthened with mussel shells.
From the deep forests near the salines northwest
to here, you can't see to find your way by the stars.
The two men dream of owning land. They work
with the weight of the sleet, bending the young
trees so that they won't stand straight again.

Sparta

He said cotton gin
and then grist and saw mills.

The farmers raised cotton on Flat Prairie,
the shuddering heads of winter wheat,
the castor beans that cracked if left
in the field too long.

      And the gin pulled hooks
on metal screens, separating
seed from fibers, repeating.
The mill planed the black jack
and post oak with steam.

The prairie went into harrows
and plows, built in town,
its name changing from Columbus
to Sparta, rival of Athens,
home of war.

      And the sun raised
what men planted from the fields
of clay loam interspersed
with sand.

North of Sparta

Through the heads of winter wheat,
the boy saw the bobolinks.
One was coal.
The other was gold.
Little soldiers, he said to them,
where is my home?
In the prairie, said the coal.
In the groves, said the gold.
And the boy, who was running
with his father's knife on his side,
heard the bobolinks rise and wheel,
saw their mouths open
in hungry song, as a little sister
first said his name, an echo
of vowels. Little soldiers, he said,
where is my home?
In the prairie, said the coal.
In the groves, said the gold.
Through the heads of the wheat,
the awns of the spikes like bayonets,
he saw the bobolinks.
Army birds, his father called them,
no need to bother to reap
these fields.

Jones and Nesbitt Mine, Coulterville

The wife looks for her breath.
Her husband mines the vein, loading
cars powered by steam. This coal
is dry, easily worked.

She will send her breath down
from Grand Cote Prairie as the current
in the shaft, a flow of wheat and small streams.

Ten men were killed in January
and six burned in December, the government
recording clothes, face and back,
face, neck, and right hand, and so on.

As she washes, she must catch her breath.
That underworld of great hot beasts
and green rotted into stone forms dust
she can't wring out of the clothes
that he strips off by the back door.

Her breath, so warm, rubs
the coal.

Roseborough Mine, Sparta

The little girl listens for her hands.
Her father has unsealed the earth
where coal drifted out of the slope,
and he has sold it.

She will throw her hands to Apollo
that he might make a border for the sun.
Then her brothers who enter the shaft
sunk into the ground, then the horses
who pull the tons of coal, will keep vision.

A hundred tons a day in the six-
foot vein, they carve under black slate
while standing on fire clay.

In the garden, the girl is listening
for her hands. The pumpkins swell
like skulls, the corn dry, dented, ready.
Her hands draw back the husks
without her even thinking.

Her hands, so cold, light
the coal.

Stripping Shovel

Raised with Adam, we came to assign names:
Silver Spade, River Queen, Mountaineer,
Ursa Major, the Gem of Egypt, and most close
to home the Captain, the largest stripping shovel
in the world. With high tensile steel,
the earthmovers stripped the coalbeds
by the millions of short tons.

We learned to bend to grab into the earth.
Old shovels blocked the stars like giants, left
as statues on the plains at Schuline. Where
they still mined at Percy, the machines' teeth
clutched in floodlights. Heavy on the land
with treads of many tons, the Captain cleared
two seams of coal at the same time,
one fifty feet above the other.

We were all taught with Adam to hold
the earth, and born from it, we returned again,
in the castles and forts we built low
near our grandfathers' gardens, in the pits
we grew up to dig on the plains,
in the nights in the kilowatts of energy
that came into our homes from deep down,
as did the sulfur that we breathed even
from coal the company cleaned.

Green Dragon

Green dragon, sudden,
grows unlike the underwater
panther here but as emerald
as clouds that foretell hail.

Arrow, arum, and the corm
was harvested out from the ground,
in between the teeth, across
the hungry tongue.

The rafter of turkeys grazes
down in the creek, where Galum,
Bonnie, Rock Fork meet,
below the circles

the looters opened, digging
down in pits to see what
they might find—a skull
so prized.

Stone Box Cemetery

Blue-eyed Mary held
the prairie by slender
taproots before being
cleared for farms, left
then to the slopes
of creeks. It was still
found by long-tongued bees
until what was a farm
became a mine
of burning stars.

Before earthmovers
took the overburden
to reveal the vein,
before plows opened
the ground to raise
the grain, snapdragons
formed colonies
under the sound
of the oaks on the flats,
true blue.

The name we give
to those who harvested
the yield of shagbark hickory,
bur, and white oak
is of a time: Woodland,
Mississippian, prehistoric.
At the cemetery of boxes
they all gathered,
in limestone and box elder
full of sugar.

Unweaved:

bottomland forest, forest
on the slope, post oak flats, prairie,
the mound on the ridge, limestone,
shale outcroppings, creek, the pits
that indicate homes, chert, and the people
who moved between, using
each before being buried.

With the terrific sound of the earth
turning inside out, awesome in tons,
the Springfield and Herrin seams
were upheaved day and night,
the light east of the County Line Road
constant, brilliant as if the heart
of a star was burning out.

The sap of the silver maple
and the weight of the river birch,
the mines stripped across
them all with heavy machines.
The panther crossed the ridge
on its way.

Under Mayapples

With mayapples, we know that spring has come,
their jump a brilliant green uncommon in wood
and stone. A rib fragment, partial cranium, shards
remain where relic hunters stirred the ground.
The shell-tempered rim where a mouth drank water
and the metacarpal that held the vessel are under
mayapples on the slope. A six-year-old walked
where glaciers left till, and the chert was worked
into useful shapes. Buried on the ridge spur
above the creek in a stone box, his grave was disturbed
by hunters, then surveyors from the expanding mine.
Offerings of shells, an antler tine, a dog canine
worn like a charm, an awl of bird bone are found.
Mayapples mean the snakes will be out soon.

Watershed

White violets, the food
of mourning doves
and mason bees, spread
over limestone boxes,
slabs fixed into forms.

There's comfort in putting a body down
under the trail of the sun.

Disturbed for what
someone might find,
the bones in the stone
box cemetery were
scattered. A child

was found resting on a woman, but it's hard
to know the original place.

Darters and sunfish,
flathead minnows
lived in Galum Creek
while farm and mine
erosion filled it with silt.

Then came the burning star
where the pit ran north-south.

The walking dragline
and its bucket from
the boom, the ropes
and metal dug
in massive motion.

What is left of a burning star?
Manganese, sulfates, silver.

They exceed
the total maximum
daily load, and the state
prepares executive
summaries and fact sheets.

Galum and Bonnie have been restored
in their approximate original locations

with meanders
and riffles. Hardwoods
and grains have been
planted to attract waterfowl
for hunters to harvest

in time. The coal company wins a prize.
Green ash and river birch

grow tall
near the state park
where snakes are so thick
they must close the road
for their crossing.

Good Times, Bad Times

It's a straight shot
but how it rolls

with the rise and fall of strip mines
between oil fields,

the underbrush
of rabbits and crushed cans.

In shaft mines, pillars
hold ceilings every so many feet,

but sometimes it's easier
to remove the earth

to get the seam.
With these rusted machines

we know we are at home,
laughing, lights off, about the hand

we can't see in front
of our own face,

some nights, the lit end
of a cigarette the only star.

If I ride the road
like a roller coaster

where coal used to be,
if I crank KSHE 95 from St. Louis

so that all the glass
shimmies in its frames,

so that my bones unroll, then I know
what it's like to be alone.

Each bone has a name,
and if we could remember,

we could be a doctor,
nurse, and go. We dream

in cemeteries, all
that's left in the center of a mine,

names of prairies and groves,
drinking Busch (and laughing

about the name), aluminum
that licks our lips

through six packs.
The sun breaks

along the shafts
of the bones every day.

IV.

Acceleration

Under unborn stars below Orion's belt,
between County Line Road and Eden,
I saw the panther once.

Curve on curve, we had practiced
acceleration in the driver's ed car there,
the Pontiac heavy on its way.

As bright as lust, the mines with legions
of lights operated at all hours. The company
built breaks of earth along

the highway so we couldn't see,
but the shine above, they were
unable to contain.

Cemeteries were left untouched, islands
of stones with names carved carefully
and ages to the day.

The panther raised its head with slowness
born of nothing to lose, eyes illuminated
beside a creek as we sped

out from a curve. Blasted and ground,
the veins of coal, abundant seams,
were yielding ton on ton,

and trains ran through town almost
every hour at night. Winter, summer,
the same, I pulsed in bed

with crossing bells and the whistles
in their minor tones, long, then short,
a code, sure as I was born.

The Fathers Who Never Seem to Speak

The fathers who never seem to speak
work at World Color Press printing comics
bright with jalopies and scarves, capes
and cityscapes. The fathers work
at Mary-Lee Gilster in white, smelling
of cake mixes, devil's food and angel's food,
work at the prisons, Mental Health
and Menard, walking in perimeters
of concertina wire, hours of cat walks,
towers. They work in the coal mines the most,
where they take the undersides of all power,
the earth we all walk on. The great stones
by their driveways are drilled perfectly through.

I creep around the houses of my friends,
not to wake their fathers on second
or third shifts. They stretch out in a room
I never see, still and great in sleep.
We keep quiet if they walk in
to watch their westerns or get beer.
They know my mom from high school,
so I'm okay with them, along the edges
of old wallpaper flowers of another
decade's days. My friends whisper,
with so much to say. We talk of dresses,
cakes, and the bright bouquets
that we will carry when we walk away.

Cadence

Our anchor of late:
the cadence of peepers,
the portion of songs by leopard,
wood, chorus frogs, on top
of each other like stars,
never stopping.
So many bodies we never see
in the ponds and creeks,

the gauze of the Milky Way
and beneath it, speech.
They are earnest in their repetition,
their throats.
Seeds are not yet formed
as our acres are in flower,
clear, deep as we sleep.
We wake to braids undone.

The ground is no longer
cold to me, and the oriole
comes to draw
her nest from thread.
How strange to learn
that we carry eggs, too,
that we have since
before we were born.

Imagine—in our ravines,
our pears, the pockets
of our hips, in the ease
of summer's coming.
We tend the lobes
of our ears, the gathers
of our sleeves,
and the cuffs of our jeans

(you'll grow into them overnight,
our mothers said, never
buying us a size that fit,
but they were right).

Flight Pattern

Little did I know that I saw her
as I came down from the sky
in a plane, circling the city,
sweeping out to the countryside
that hosts the city, cameo on the breast
of the land, carved as a lady's face,
neck, and breast.

I moved around like I-270, built
when I was young through ancient
plazas and graves, crews lifting
away pottery for themselves, tearing
through earth around and near
Cahokia, the mounds, the racetrack,
the Jarrot house.

I swung over Alton where my father
served as jury foreman for a trial
about racetrack corruption, over East St. Louis
where trash bloomed on the streets
with eggs thrown at cars, empty-mouthed
red brick buildings with trees reaching
tall as stories from the roofs.

Over the glacial plains I circled
toward my old home, Randolph County,
the quilted pattern of fields
in and out of harvest, opened
again to seed. I crossed the dark ways
of hardwoods interlocking,
over strip mines and forests

and the silver hem of the river,
over houses with evergreen windblocks
planted to the northwest, certain
they would hold back winter

from each farmhouse. On silos
farmers framed stars in wire
with white lights in December.

Each city was a meeting
of crossing routes in streetlights
and distant broken roads of crows
and trains of coal and grain.
The circles of Monsanto
huddled down, refining near
the chain of rocks that broke

the river's easy sailing, pushing
barges into a canal, past the bridge
of the same name where teenagers died
of gunshot wounds and Eads Bridge
that a tornado once disassembled.
I came closer, to crow-bellied earth
from the glaciers' grinding weight,

to crow-eyed coal from old opulent marshes.
The pioneers first knew coal when
lightning hit the bluff stone and it
kept burning. Below, Madame Jarrot
held her arms out to each side, her hair
and cape still defined, her eyes
weathered away on her stone.

I saw her, Julie and her generations
of slaves, the brick and black walnut
mansion, December 1845 *Jarrot
v Jarrot* ending Illinois' black code,
*Julia Beauvais of Ste. Genevieve,
originally of Kaskaskia*, who cried
on her wedding day when she left home.

Venus

Don't let your mother see,
my cousin says, pressing
the lipstick into my palm.

So I run outside, west
into Venus sky, bands
of chaff in the air, the dust

of wheat from acres all around
our farm. Upriver, from Kaskaskia
to Cahokia, combines

operate still by headlight. They
give tonight a color of wine, the inner
folds of a rose.

I study the gift in such afterglow:
a few inches of white plastic,
soft point, lovely arrow.

Run west, run into Venus.
With the hook above the mouth,
the full slope under,

like the river the mouth,
her voice returns rain
to ocean and back again.

What is that on your face?
I come back in with sunset
all over me.

Tongue of Vines

Swaddled in bricks and beams hewn from the forest,
his sons and daughters heard the pileated woodpecker
uttering a tongue of vines as thick as slow water,
Okaw. The Kaskaskia had been west thirty years by then,
but his children knew the story of when he was seven,
when the chief came to his father for his hunting dogs.

They wouldn't go, so his father sent him along, through forests
of walnut and the last wolves, the buffalo by then all bones,
along rivers and creeks of black willow, sedge, foxes,
riverbank grape. His mother was gone with his birth
back in Tennessee. The Kaskaskia told a story of a woman
who loved a painted turtle like a man and became

one herself, soft-shelled. Dark green as the forest,
the turtles basked in the slow water, designed
in the black, red, yellow the Kaskaskia wore.
Swimming backwards, the male brushed his claws
across the female's face. The boy spoke to the dogs,
commanding them with his father's escalating call.

The Kaskaskia brought him home from the forest
in a few days. We still see the birds sometimes, white
sudden under wings when they fly from the dead trees,
having dug deep into the wood, red crests ringing.
They feed their young until the fall, growing yellow
eyes over the rivers and creeks of black willows.

The Kaskaskia village plowed under, the forests
profuse with vines about the father's falling house,
we hear them drumming out their acres even now.

Wish to His Branch

He tends the earth and sends wood into wagons like the old constellation
in the summer sky. Soft as the night in June, he flails his wheat. Crows
follow to eat the grubs turned up in his furrows.
                                    From their shape, in purple reasons,
the grapes are crushed from their skins. His blend of juice and barrel
moves in a full body that he stores under his house where brick joins soil.

Stairs ascend in their house as the trees that they once were,
three stories worn smoother each year by bare soles and boots. To her
ten-year-old eye, the forest defies winter's snowfall, soldiering in butternut
brown, just as her father defies the revenue officers who took his wine.

Like her mother and older sisters, she uses the stick by the back door
to push out snakes that try to slide inside. Nights, they talk of war,
their confederacy, what the future holds in store.

She watches her father fashion a wagon tongue and put lynch pins
in the wheels. A man has dreams for his children, the wish
to his branch, the cutting from his vine.
                                      The land gives
no grace, nor does the Lord our God if we forget our way.
In the spring house where the milk keeps cool, old snake skins
lessen into feathers of scales, the new snakes rapid, away.

Lines and Glass Insulators

The earth doesn't love us. Who'd think that?
We walk the railroad tracks
in summertime, tar seeping out from the ties,
creosote, and waves of lines
held by glass insulators on the poles
send what is spoken
about the trains in sparkling rows.

A dog barks into afternoon, and sisters croon
about a man with a slow hand.
We read about our signs, told by star time.
Surely they are right,
lions and scales and what is preordained.
A good man would understand
without words how to move.

Down the tracks in the sticking sun and back again,
the dog's still going, the radio
playing, left on in the grass, antenna silver
catching the stations from across the river.
The junior who lives across the street
has opened his hood, sweet
lemonade in our hands that she

would give him. His chin
is in the engine. The dog extends
to the length of his chain, steps
along his edge of packed hard
yard. We can't help what the stars
say we'll be. She says some day he'll
love me. I just wish he'd hurry.

Myocarditis

The dauphine, queen-to-be, is a broken valentine.
In podunk Illinois, you don't blink your eyes,
driving through a one-horse-town. The railroad crossing
holds no gates, just Xs on posts where soft coal is running
on the Missouri-Pacific line. It strides by Butter Creek, corn,
and St. Pius Church. The town is named for the man
who brought the railroad here before going to jail, a banker
who died from an inflammation of the muscles of his heart.

A cat walks the tracks, perfect on the rail, a steady flame.
The dauphine uses oil to darken her skin, rubbing it in, belly
up to the sun in a lawnchair. She squints in the glare.
The antenna holds out a crow's foot on the roof, stretching
to the city, tuning to the never-empty air. Blackbirds nod
in the acres. The dauphine dreams of becoming anything.
Her father will pay for college for her brother, but not
for her, a waste, since girls just get married anyways.

Males sport bright shoulders above the dull females.
Males sing again and again, while females lace their homes
from what they find low in the fields. The dauphine reads
her mother's magazines: the breakthroughs in hair care,
when he breaks your heart, what you should do.
Out of the blue, the English prince chose his future queen.
At the altar the princess doesn't say she will obey.

Cathedral Train

She is meandering like the river past us, violets
crushed above her eyes with pearl. Vibrant,
skittering, beads run the seams and down
her back into her train. It sweeps the linoleum
of the bar like a cathedral floor, and the miners
raise their bottles to the groom, who was drunk
even before.

Marissa, Freeburg, St. Libory, we must stop
at every bar between the church and the reception hall.
That's the way, and we obey. The best man
helps her climb onto a stool at the bar, and her heels
dangle off her toes at the rung. She glows in satin
like the bolts her mother cuts at the dress factory
into gowns

for days like now. Seed pearls and sequins
mix a radiant clutter around her breasts.
The miners grind down their ash in the trays
on the tables and don't say much that we can hear.
In the foundation of her face, I see a child
pressed against a front screen door.
I hear

my mother say, don't do that, you'll bust
out the wire, where do you think you're going
anyway? We considered sweep or cathedral train,
the sweetheart neck, empire or princess
shape. We picked our groom from folds
of notebook pages, divided into triangles
and counted down

by random numbers that we chose.
The first of us to have her day, the bride
glides around the tables on her way
out the door, like a small bit of stone caught

in a mine's light. We work our way
from church to reception hall, across prairies
turned bottom up

for coal, and stop again outside another plain
white building with a Budweiser sign.
Inside, the only colors are the bottles of hard
liquor behind the bar, the neon signs, the posters
for the Cardinals and a girl to the side.
These men are used to dark places.
They look up

once and then don't pay us any mind.
We know by now to smile without
keeping their eye. Soybeans rattle
in their shells, and pumpkins
swell like the sun caught, a rind thick
into its many strung seeds
inside.

Galette des Rois

As the fibers
in blown glass,
like Alabama
tides, yellow fever,
the orphans abide.
They dream
of being brides.

Gabrielle
from St. Denis
sails on the *Pelican*
from France
with the other girls,
to Mobile
by way of Havana.
She is one
of the last to marry.

The wheat can't
grow with the rust
from the heat,
the humidity
of the bayou,
so they move
the colony upriver.

Farther beyond
in Illinois country,
her son engineers
Fort de Chartres
from river stone
in the limestone heart
of the continent,
for lead and wheat,
the powder magazine.

Her granddaughter
marries a fur trader,
who becomes
lieutenant governor.
The rivers advance
past his walnut bed
and hand-pressed panes.

Don't ever think
that water dreams.
The river rolls
and will not sleep,
but each woman moves
as steam rising.
In the galette des rois,
one small seed
is found.

Cerulean

Warblers pull on full
thistles, swaying over
black hickory nuts busted
to dust on the ground.
The male and female
fasten parts of blue,
green, gold on the bluff
above the river.

      Belly down in the grass
      in the earthworks
      of Fort Kaskaskia, a child
      waits in hide and seek. You won't find her.
      Here comes the surge
      of a train along the river. Here burns the thrum
      of a barge between the shores.
      She knows each curve
      of moat and ramparts,
      each step down to the river,
      the roots of the hickory
      uncurled.

The threatened
birds feed in morning,
in the open eyes of crushed
sky. Born of bark
and grass bound
in webs, the warblers
eat, faces in thistles
to the eyes.

Low in Spirits

Ice on the river, like unworked chert,
slides in fractures of fine grains,
bright as her own name
that she gives to her first child,
born in February. The sky
keeps close as a grooved axe.

She hears tales of the outlaw
who lived in this garrison before,
how he dove fingers first
into a man's eyes
and would have put them out.

The baby stirs in sleep, eyes
shut but looking side to side.

Below them, tribes cross
the river from time to time.
Her husband writes
that she should *cheer up*
and try to be lively.

Snow like heavy feathers is falling again
over the hundred men in the regiment,
over her, the officer's wife. Clarissa, Clara—the bright
wakes, suddenly more
hungry than anyone can bear.

The Height Is the Only Place that Will Do

Like glass this place held dreams
of a safe space, *commanded
from no point and which will command all.*

A cannon was fired from here to make a point
but the first fort was never completely built,
the cannon taken down to fortify the town,
the place scavenged for wood and iron.

Trees grew from earthworks,
our home base in tag, so strictly mowed, we ran
barefoot. We knew
shade by our feet, our eyes closed.

Men from the university found what was fine (creamware,
pearlware with feathered edge, shells
cobalt blue) and what was coarse (redware,
stoneware, violet
inside, the outside, salt-glazed brown),
the rose-head nails,
brass kettle sheets, lead musket balls,
the spall gunflint.

We hunted Easter eggs by the tombstones
removed to here as the river took the town.
Men guarded the prison below us, built
of Palestine limestone. Under that, the limestone

run through with shale bore Menard's name,
weathered smooth and when broken, blue gray,
beds of old seas built from such small
bodies we couldn't imagine.

Night, songs of leopard frogs.
Summer tightened its throat as we ran
out of our parents' sight.

Relict of a Husband, Daughter of a General

Danger, our mothers say,
is in earthquakes that will
someday come. We mark
their words and run

under clouds of flint
and fire steel where a baby
was born in the garrison
and took her mother's name.

Her father died young
and her husband (a president's son),
so that *her mind was ever
afterward clouded*

until she died. Her mother
raised her six boys and girls,
and they also had bad luck:
one struck by lightning,

one killed by Indians
out west, two dead
by cholera. One girl
bore the general's name

Zebulon, like a man.
Let me try my hand
at singing a more
luminous story.

>   Clara, any daughter knows these mountains
>   are in love with you, Pike's Peak out west
>   and the Ozarks here in Illinois. *Laugh at half
>   the world's folly and despite the envy of the balance,*
>   your husband wrote. When he was killed
>   in war, you wore black ever since, seeming tall,

> but first, when you were *very lonesome* over
> Kaskaskia, your daughter was born.

A baby camped
in Easter snow, morning
torn like stars from pages
of clear sky. For her mother,

like all of us, she crawled.
She marked the ways
of wood warblers,
how the mother

drops below the nest
before she flies,
her throat a trill of Zs,
bright heaven, sky.

No father wants
an army life for his girl,
so we run from home.
Our words are lost in fire.

Judgment is coming,
but until then, we hide
in the earthworks
in our time.

Ismenian Dragon

Is a constellation bigger than the house, than the state?
My son leans into my answer like a hard turn. I describe
the lion's size, measure the bear's back, and he is excited
that there's a dragon, too. It curls around the sky, waiting,
where he will piece together its scales. He draws lines
and dots, alive in his mind pacing the sky, sure as I'm sitting
by his side. There is the brother in search of his sister,
taken by the gods, and the fragments of the dragon
that he killed, the teeth he planted so that armies rose
to help him build Thebes. I tell my son of home,
the running slave, the Mississippi with white ash and clay.
The dragon was killed guarding the water from a spring.
His body of venom, the spots on his back glitter around
us even now, like men born armed, upset from the ground.

Ourania, Pandemos, Apostrophia

These are the stories of the water's ways, the Nile,
and Mississippi, and of more than one town that holds
the same name, Thebes, filling the footprints of myths
and geology. Above the river canes, rushes, marshes,
trains run without stopping so that the town decays
in vibrations of timber and stone. Three Aphrodites,
prows cut off the ships of a prince and left by his bride,
remind us of pure love, sexual love, and one to keep
crime in love away. And I know this place in Illinois was
named for Egypt, but what the muses said at the wedding
at Thebes in Greece holds true: *what is beautiful is loved, what
is not beautiful is not loved*—the slaves sold down the river,
the effortless glide of snakes, how they hear movement
with the muscles and bones of their lower jaw.

Hephaestus's Fire

On her wedding day, the dark-eyed girl wore a necklace
from her grandparents. A two-headed serpent studded
with diamonds clasped an eagle between gold double tongues.
Later, she and her husband were turned into snakes,
winding in dust, a curse the craftsman gave for an old affair
or as a way to show that the innocent suffer as much
as the guilty. We wreathe the heads of the dead in sarsaparilla
as we've been taught. We wreathe a bride and groom in dianthus,
milkstar, snowdrops. Be true of voice. Come back, to tend
the fields, to work the waters of the shores, to move the sands
of the east and west banks. Long ago someone wrote our names
on the lintel over this door. From the courthouse, we have a most
far-reaching view. The sun is setting, children, and falling all
over you. This is the verse that went through our lips.

Notes

"Marie Louise" quotes from a letter from Governor Carondelet to Lieutenant Governor Trudeau, found in Carl J. Ekberg's *Colonial Ste. Genevieve*.

"Marie Scypion" quotes from William E. Foley's article "Slave Freedom Suits Before Dred Scott: The Case of Marie Jean Scypion's Descendants," published in *Missouri Historical Review*. This poem follows the form of René Char's "Les Trois Sœurs" ("The Three Sisters") and contains echoes of that poem as well.

"Thebes Courthouse" quotes from the courthouse historical marker located off Route 3 in Thebes, Illinois.

"Thou has brought a vine out of Egypt:" quotes from Psalms 80:8-19, KJV.

"Watershed" quotes from "Mining Reclamation Success – Burning Star," an online report available via the Mineral Information Institute website.

"Good Times, Bad Times" takes its title from Led Zeppelin's debut album *Led Zeppelin*. Echoes of that song are also found in that poem.

"Flight Pattern" quotes from *The Romantic Story of Cahokia*, a book available online via the Illinois Bottomland Explorer Archive.

"Lines and Glass Insulators" echoes "Slow Hand," the advance single for the Pointer Sisters' album *Black & White*.

"Low in Spirits" takes its title and quote from the letters of Zebulon Pike, army officer and explorer. Quotes in "Relict of a Husband, Daughter of a General" also come from these letters and W. Eugene Hollon's *The Lost Pathfinder: Zebulon Montgomery Pike*.

"The Height Is the Only Place that Will Do" takes its title and quote from correspondence between François Saucier, engineer, and Commandant M. de McCarty, included in Southern Illinois Studies No. 17 *Preliminary Archeological Research at Fort Kaskaskia*.

"Ourania, Pandemos, Apostrophia" quotes from fragments of Theognis, and echoes of this poet are also found in "Hephaestus's Fire."

"Tornado at Chester," "Sparta," "North of Sparta," "Jones and Nesbitt Mine, Coulterville," and "Roseborough Mine, Sparta" follow the forms of Federico García Lorca.

Angie Macri was born and raised in southern Illinois, where her mother's family has lived for more than two centuries. After studying at the University of Arkansas, she has worked in Arkansas as a technical writer and educator. An Arkansas Arts Council fellow, she lives in Hot Springs.

Her poems have been included in *Arts & Letters*, *Best New Poets*, *Cimarron Review*, *A Face to Meet the Faces: An Anthology of Contemporary Persona Poetry*, *New Madrid*, *The Southern Review*, *The Spoon River Poetry Review*, and other journals. Her chapbook *Fear Nothing of the Future or the Past*, which works with H.D.'s *Helen in Egypt*, the mounds around Helena, Arkansas, and the paintings of Carroll Cloar, was published by Finishing Line Press. *Underwater Panther* is her first full-length book publication.

Links to publications, events, and more can be found at angiemacri.wordpress.com.